HAUNTED OR HOAX?

HAUNTED AT SEA

JAIME WINTERS

CRABTREE
PUBLISHING COMPANY
WWW.CRABTREEBOOKS.COM

HAUNTED OR HOAX?

Author: Jaime Winters

Editors: Edward O'Connor, Marcia Abramson, Petrice Custance

Photo research: Melissa McClellan

Cover/interior design: T.J. Choleva

Proofreader: Lorna Notsch

Production coordinator and prepress technician: Tammy McGarr

Print coordinator: Katherine Berti

Consultant: Susan Demeter-St. Clair Paranormal Studies & Inquiry

Written and produced for Crabtree Publishing by BlueAppleWorks Inc.

Photographs & Illustrations
Cover illustration: T.J Choleva (background image: Melkor3D/Shutterstock ; front image: Kiselev Andrey Valerevich/Shutterstock); Title page illustration: Joshua Avramson (background image: Melkor3D/Shutterstock; front image: Netfalls Remy Musser /Shutterstock)
Shutterstock.com: © Login (page backgrounds); © Morphart Creation (p. 4 bottom left); © Sergey Mikhaylov (p. 4 bottom); © Kiselev Andrey Valerevich (p. 5 bottom left); © PLRANG ART (p. 5 bottom); © cherezoff (p. 5, 17, 21, 27 middle); © Lotus_studio (p. 5 right); © AridOcean (p. 6 left); © irabel8 (p. 6–7 bottom); © tj-rabbit(p. 8–9 bottom); © Ivan Cholakov (p. 9); © Rainer Lesniewski (p. 9 top right); © cpaulfell (p. 10 left); © Ursatii (p. 10 right); © Peter Hermes Furian (p. 11 right middle); © Igor Samoiliuk (p. 11 bottom); Ensuper (p. 11, 19 middle); © Triff (p. 11, 15, 17, 19, 21, 25, 27, 29 sidebar); © Allen McDavid Stoddard (p. 12 top right); © Volina (p. 14 top left); © Ruslan Gus (p. 14–15 bottom); © Aleksandr Abrosimov (p. 15, 25, 29 middle); © Kristina Vackova (p. 15 bottom middle); © Fiona Ayerst (p. 16 bottom); © Andrea Izzotti (p. 16 bottom right); © Dean Drobot (p. 17 bottom); © cherezoff (p. 17 middle); © Andrey Yurlov (p. 20–21 bottom); © Nerthuz (p. 21 left); © Krivosheev Vitaly (p. 22 bottom); Digital Storm (p. 28 top right); © Kestutis Zitinevicius (p. 28 bottom right)
Creative Commons: Awgrasso (p. 4 top right); Anynobody (p. 8 left); RuthAS (p. 9 top left); Erik Oberg/Island Conservation (p. 14 top right); Anagoria (p. 18 bottom left); Wellcome Collection (p. 18 right); Chris 73 / Wikimedia Commons (p. 18–19 bottom); Sanfranman59 (p. 21 right)
Public Domain: Sir George Chalmers (p. 5 bottom right); Gift of J. Pierpont Morgan, 1900 (p. 6 right); Photographed by Sargent/United States Naval History and Heritage Command (p. 7 top right); p. 8 top right; US Navy)p. 8 right middle); Ocean Explorer/NOAA (p. 12 top left, 12 top right); U.S. Fish and Wildlife Service Headquarters (p. 14 bottom left); Susan White/USFWS (p. 16 top right); John S. Johnston (p. 20 bottom left); Illustrated London News (p. 20 top right); Iziko William Fehr Collection (p.25 left); Aldus Books London (p. 25 right); Royal Collection (p. 26 top right); Charles Temple Dix (p. 26 bottom); Ludolf Bakhuizen (p. 27 bottom); p. 27 top right; P. T. Barnums (p. 29 bottom right)
Joshua Avramson p. 12 bottom, p. 23, p. 24–25 (background image Unholy Vault Designs/Shutterstock; front image: Kiselev Andrey Valerevich/Shutterstock; front right Tithi Luadthong/Shutterstock)
Carlyn Iverson p. 13 bottom, p. 22 left

Library and Archives Canada Cataloguing in Publication

Winters, Jaime, author
Haunted at sea / Jaime Winters.

(Haunted or hoax?)
Includes index.
Issued in print and electronic formats.
ISBN 978-0-7787-4638-6 (hardcover).--
ISBN 978-0-7787-4644-7 (softcover).--
ISBN 978-1-4271-2057-1 (HTML)

1. Haunted places--Juvenile literature. 2. Ocean--Folklore. 3. Ghosts--Juvenile literature. I. Title.

BF1486.W46 2018 j133.1'22 C2017-907792-9
C2017-907793-7

Library of Congress Cataloging-in-Publication Data

CIP available at the Library of Congress

Crabtree Publishing Company
www.crabtreebooks.com 1-800-387-7650

Printed in the U.S.A./032018/BG20180202

Published in Canada
Crabtree Publishing
616 Welland Ave.
St. Catharines, Ontario
L2M 5V6

Published in the United States
Crabtree Publishing
PMB 59051
350 Fifth Avenue, 59th Floor
New York, New York 10118

Published in the United Kingdom
Crabtree Publishing
Maritime House
Basin Road North, Hove
BN41 1WR

Published in Australia
Crabtree Publishing
3 Charles Street
Coburg North
VIC, 3058

CONTENTS

MYSTERIES OF DEEP WATERS

In 1493, the explorer Christopher Columbus wrote in his journal that he had spotted three mermaids. He described the creatures as "not half as beautiful as they are painted." It is now thought that Columbus actually saw three manatees!

Oceans flow and roar over more than 70 percent of Earth, yet much of the deep has not been explored. No wonder **myths**, **legends**, and monsters seem to rise up regularly from the mysterious seas!

Creeps of the Deep

The ocean can seem frightening because it is so deep, wide, and full of strange and sometimes scary creatures. In the past, many sailors reported seeing gigantic sea monsters with long arms that could wrap around a ship and pull it down. They said these creatures, called **leviathans**, could squeeze a sailor to death. They also talked of giant squids, singing **mermaids**, and many other strange creeps of the deep.

Sea monsters were considered real in the ***Age of Discovery****. They were even drawn on some sailors' maps.*

Tales of the Paranormal

Sailors also brought back stories of ghosts, **demons**, **cursed** islands, and **paranormal** spirits. They told stories that made people's blood run cold. Imagine being on a ship and seeing another ship coming right at you and then vanishing before it hits your ship. At first, these spooky stories seem to have no scientific explanation. When we read them, we have to ask: Can science find a reason for this, or is it truly a haunted story?

*Sailors of the past did not know what caused storms and other disasters on voyages. So they turned to myths and legends to explain the dangers that threatened every sailor, including hurricanes, **typhoons**, and **waterspouts**.*

DEADLY SCURVY

During the Age of Discovery (from the 1400s to the 1700s) Europeans began crossing the oceans on long voyages. Sea monsters may not have been a real danger, but scurvy was. This deadly disease killed as many as two million sailors. We now know it is caused by a lack of Vitamin C. Scurvy breaks apart the human body. It forms blood blisters on the skin, rots the gums, shatters bones, and eventually, destroys the brain. In fact, sailors with scurvy might easily have been mistaken for ghosts or demons themselves.

Dr. James Lind used scientific research to fight scurvy. In 1747, he proved that citrus fruits such as oranges, lemons, and limes could ward off or even cure the disease.

HAUNTINGS IN THE BERMUDA TRIANGLE

Strange things happen in a patch of deep water in the Atlantic Ocean known as the Bermuda Triangle. More than 500 years ago, sailors were calling the area the Sea of Lost Ships. There is a long list of ships that have disappeared after entering the area. Is something evil lurking in the Bermuda Triangle, or can it all be easily explained?

DID YOU KNOW?

Explorer Christopher Columbus sailed through the Bermuda Triangle in 1492. In his log, he wrote that the ship's compass stopped working and that a ball of fire crashed into the sea there.

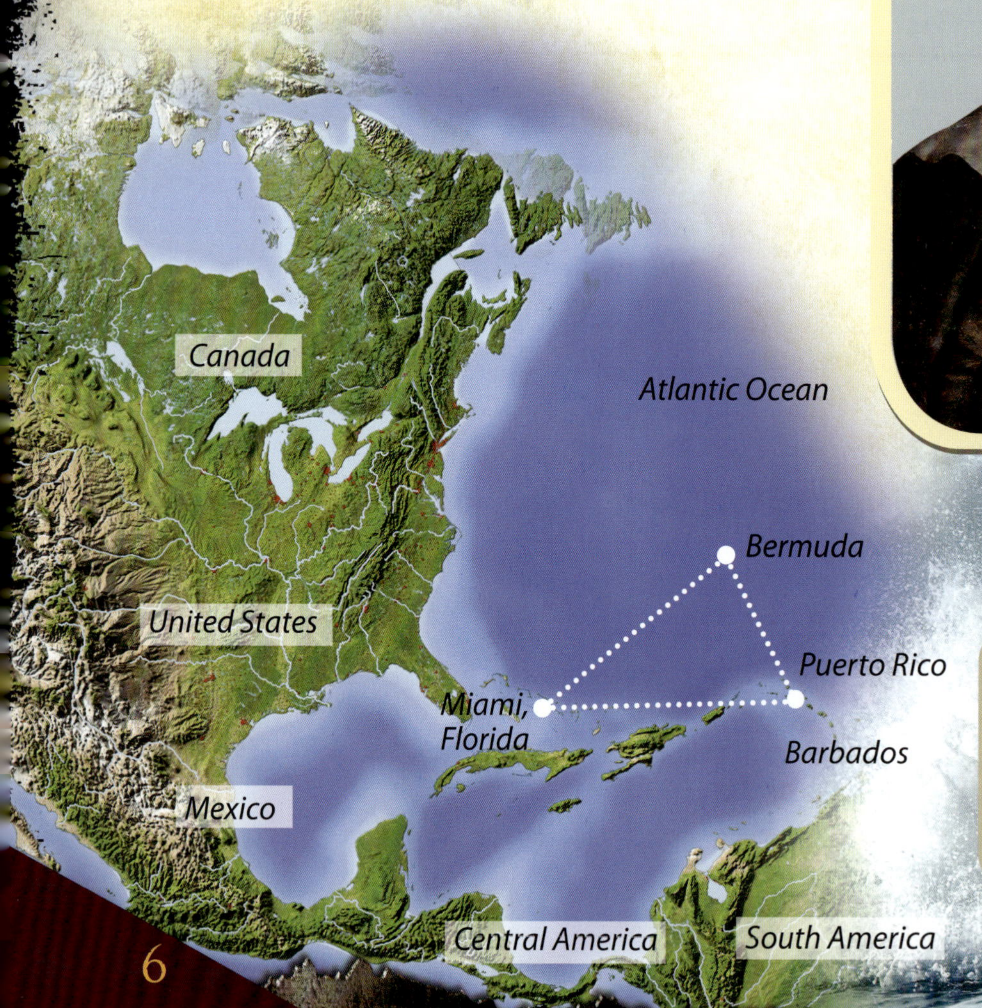

Connect the dots: The area within the dotted lines connecting Bermuda, Miami, and Puerto Rico is known as the Bermuda Triangle.

Cyclops Lost at Sea

In 1918, the United States Ship (USS) *Cyclops*, named after the one-eyed giant from myths, left Barbados for Baltimore (see map on page 6). The U.S. Navy ship carried a heavy load. Unfortunately, its fierce name didn't provide safe passage for the large ship and crew of 309. Even though the *Cyclops* had the latest radio equipment, the ship still vanished somewhere inside the Bermuda Triangle. The ship went down without making a single radio call for help.

Several years before World War I (1914–1918), the United States Navy built the USS Cyclops *to carry coal and other* ***mineral ores****.*

Without a Trace

The U.S. Navy searched for months but found no survivors or wreckage. Searchers could find no explanation for the ship's odd disappearance. Some people thought a giant octopus might have risen up from the sea, wrapped its arms around the ship, and yanked her under. Others said a German submarine might have destroyed or captured the *Cyclops*, because Germany and the United States were at war in 1918. However, after the war ended, German records showed that none of the country's subs were in the area at the time the *Cyclops* went missing.

WAS WEATHER TO BLAME?

Weather can change quickly in the Bermuda Triangle. The Cyclops *left Barbados on March 4 and was expected in Baltimore on March 13. Before she arrived in Barbados, the captain reported one engine wasn't working. Records also show that a strong wind struck off the coast of Virginia on March 10, when the* Cyclops *may have been sailing by. So some people think a combination of engine trouble, a heavy load, and strong wind may have sunk the* Cyclops*.*

Stranger Things

In 1941, during World War II, two sister ships of the *Cyclops*—*Proteus* and *Nereus*—mysteriously vanished in the Bermuda Triangle within one month of each other. Again, no survivors or wreckage were ever found. Four years later, five Navy planes disappeared. This only added to the area's reputation as a site where strange things happened.

Like the Cyclops, Nereus *(top) and* Proteus *(bottom) carried heavy loads of mineral ores. Could this have had something to do with their disappearances?*

The Mystery Deepens

In 1945, five planes took off from Florida on a routine training exercise called "Flight 19." Partway through the flight, the lead pilot radioed air traffic control that his compasses weren't working and the planes were flying in the wrong direction. Just hours later, the five planes and their crews had disappeared. Two seaplanes took to the air to search for them, but one of those seaplanes also vanished. Many think it exploded shortly after takeoff.

Missing Planes Never Found

The Navy sent more than 300 boats and aircraft to look for Flight 19 and the missing seaplane. They found nothing. Investigators said Flight 19 was lost for "causes or reasons unknown." Then, in 1949, two passenger planes, the *Star Tiger* and *Star Ariel*, also vanished over the Bermuda Triangle. Some people began to suspect that the area acted like a paranormal gateway to another world.

THE MICHIGAN TRIANGLE

Lake Michigan has its own triangle where spooky things happen. In 1891, a sailing ship, her crew of seven, and cargo of lumber disappeared without a trace there. Then, in 1950, Northwest Airlines Flight 2501 crashed in the Michigan Triangle. The plane's 58 passengers and crew were never seen again.

The Star Tiger *was a British passenger plane like the one pictured above. It carried a crew of six and 25 passengers on the day it vanished.*

DID YOU KNOW?

The investigation into the cause of the *Star Tiger* disappearance lasted 11 days. The final report said:

" .... What happened in this case will never be known and the fate of *Star Tiger* must remain an unsolved mystery."

Strange Things Pile Up

Cyclops, *Star Tiger*, *Star Ariel*, and Flight 19 aren't the only ships and planes to vanish in the Bermuda Triangle. Hundreds of other ships and planes have gone missing. As the unsolved cases piled up, investigators, scientists, and even regular citizens began to search for a solution to the mystery.

DID YOU KNOW?

The seafloor under the Bermuda Triangle is about 20,000 feet (6,100 m) deep. Any wreckage that is down there will likely remain—undisturbed and undetected.

Theory for Your Thoughts

In 1964, a newspaper reporter named Vincent Gaddis first used the term "Bermuda Triangle" to identify the area where so many ships and planes had vanished. The name caught on. Soon, several books were published that offered many weird theories to explain the strange events. One writer believed the missing ships and planes were sucked through a gate to a different time period. Another thought that maybe space aliens had captured them. A more recent writer has suggested that a fire crystal from the lost city of **Atlantis** may have somehow zapped them.

NATURAL CAUSES?

Scientists have answers that are much different from these far-out ***theories****. They believe that natural causes can explain many disappearances in the Bermuda Triangle. These causes include waterspouts, which are tornadoes that form over water, and undersea earthquakes. Another possible reason is local variations in Earth's* ***magnetic field****. This could cause a ship's compass to give wrong readings.*

Pure Mystery or Plain Ordinary?

Larry Kusche, a librarian, investigated the Bermuda Triangle in 1975. He came to a conclusion that surprised many people—that there's really no mystery at all. For example, he found that some disappearances happened during storms, even though calm seas had been reported. Accident records kept by the insurance company Lloyd's of London and the U.S. Coast Guard support his findings. In fact, the percentage of ships and planes lost in the area is the same as anywhere else in the world. Today, many scientists agree with Kusche that the mysteries of the Bermuda Triangle can be blamed on plain old bad weather and human error.

THE DRAGON'S TRIANGLE

According to ancient legends, dragons once lived in this triangular area off the coast of Japan. Today, the ocean area has a reputation for the paranormal just like the Bermuda Triangle. A number of boats, ships, and planes have vanished there without explanation. What's more, the Dragon's Triangle is also known for electronic equipment problems, as well as ghost ship and alien spacecraft sightings.

LOOK AT THE EVIDENCE

*As you read through these cases of disappearing ships and planes in the Bermuda Triangle, did you spot any solid **evidence** for the causes behind them? Or any **eyewitness** accounts? What do you think is causing strange things to go on there?*

LOST IN THE SARGASSO SEA

Just next door to the Bermuda Triangle in the Atlantic Ocean lies a wide stretch of water called the Sargasso Sea. Its calm waters are covered with brown mats of sargassum weeds that gave the sea its name. But the Sargasso Sea struck terror into sailors' hearts long before anyone heard of the Bermuda Triangle.

Lines of sargassum seaweed can stretch for many miles.

Dead Calm

Forget winds that howl, storms that rage, and waves that soar. The Sargasso Sea is so calm, it's spooky. In 1492, when explorer Christopher Columbus and his crew sailed into the sea, they got scared they might never leave. They relied on wind and rushing water currents to travel. They found little of either in an area about the same size as the United States. They worried they would get stuck and die of thirst or starvation.

In the days of sailing ships, crew members feared being slowed down or even trapped by sargassum seaweed.

Dead Ship Sailing

Columbus and his ships made it through the Sargasso Sea. The *Rosalie* was not so lucky. In 1840, another ship found her drifting near the Bahamas. Her sails were set, her cargo intact, but every crew member and passenger had vanished. Sailors also found the *James B. Chester* in 1857 floating in the sea with no crew on board. In 1881, the *Ellen Austin* came across an abandoned schooner in the same area. The captain sent a small crew aboard to sail the ship into **port**. Two days later, the substitute crew had also vanished.

LOOK AT THE EVIDENCE

Does some evil force lurk in the Sargasso Sea that dooms ships and their crews? Does any evidence exist to suggest that paranormal activity may play a role? Are there eyewitness accounts to back up such conclusions? Could nature be at work here instead? What do you think?

SHIP GRAVEYARD

Tons of ship wreckage and other trash drift into the Sargasso Sea. Some people say this is evidence that something in the weedy water has destroyed the ships. Legends describe sea monsters and killer plants whose tendrils grow in seconds around becalmed ships. However, experts say ocean currents that surround the Sargasso carry many things into it. Then the incredibly still water traps it all there.

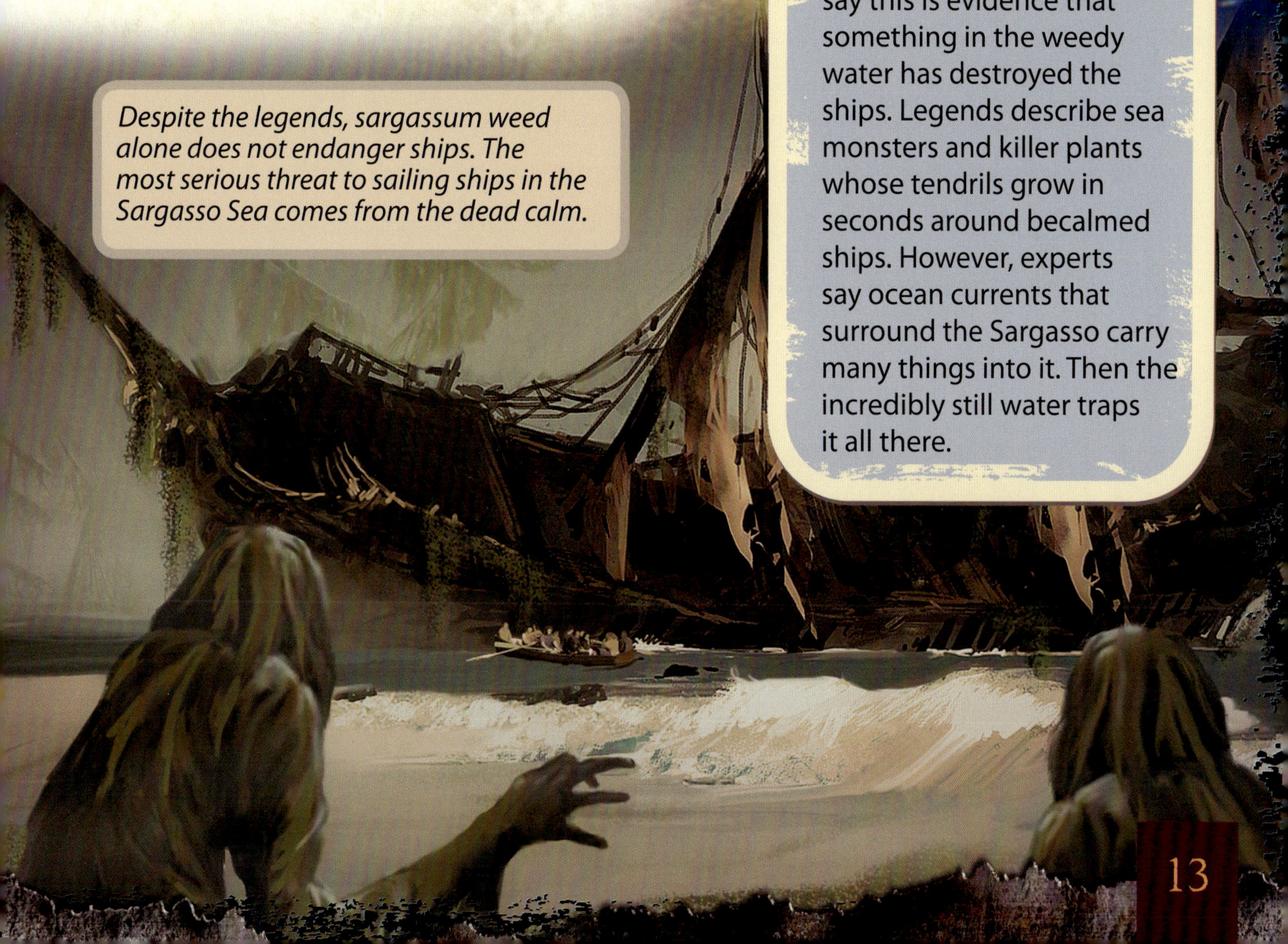

Despite the legends, sargassum weed alone does not endanger ships. The most serious threat to sailing ships in the Sargasso Sea comes from the dead calm.

HAUNTED PARADISE

Imagine a place on Earth that's tropically lush and beautiful but poses a deadly threat to anyone who dares to visit. A place so creepy, it seems like a living being with a mind and will of its own! Welcome to Palmyra **Atoll** in the South Pacific Ocean.

Palmyra Atoll is still a tropical wilderness where no one lives. The islands lie about 1,000 miles (1,600 km) south of Hawaii.

Heck of a Discovery

Whether or not it has a mind of its own, Palmyra does have a body, and a dangerous one at that. The atoll consists of a **coral reef** surrounding several islands. In 1798, Edmund Fanning, captain of the American ship *Betsy*, was nearing the atoll when a feeling of doom woke him three times in one night. Going on deck, he spotted the reef just in time to keep the *Betsy* from crashing into it. Though Fanning reported the reef in the ship's log, he failed to file his report right away. So credit for the atoll's discovery goes to Cornelius Sawle, captain of the USS *Palmyra*, which got stuck on the reef in 1802.

Palmyra's islands are covered with coconut palms. The coral reef is part of a National Wildlife Refuge. Many fish and sea turtles live amid the brightly colored corals.

Coral Menace

The coral reef around Palmyra soon became known as a danger to ships. Some sailors said the reef suddenly popped out of the water in areas that looked coral-free just seconds before. Others said they saw glowing lights flit around the atoll like ghosts. Some even said the sea around Palmyra was filled with monsters and that many ships that went there were never seen or heard from again. In 1855, for example, a whaling ship crashed onto the reef. Investigators failed to find any wreckage or a single survivor.

INCA GOLD

Perhaps the most famous shipwreck on Palmyra's reef was that of a pirate ship that looted the Spanish merchant vessel *Esperanza*. The *Esperanza* was sailing from Peru in 1816. The ship was loaded with tons of gold and silver the Spanish had taken from the **Incas**. Not long after seizing the *Esperanza*'s treasure and crew, the pirate ship crashed onto Palmyra's reef. Survivors managed to load some of the treasure onto rafts and transfer it to the island. After a year, the men felt they had no hope of rescue. They buried their treasure and tried to escape on rafts. Only one sailor survived. He was rescued by a whaling ship but died in a hospital in San Francisco. The treasure? According to legend, it remains buried on Palmyra to this day.

Palymra's coconut palms provide food and shelter for the world's largest ***crustacean****. The coconut crab can grow to more than three feet (1 m) in length and live 60 years!*

DID YOU KNOW?

A coral reef is like a city under the sea. It starts with tiny creatures called polyps. They secrete a stony substance that they use to build little "apartments" for shelter. Over time, these individual shelters grow into "apartment buildings" that can hold whole colonies of polyps.

Not every shipwreck on Palmyra's reef vanished like the whaling ship. Many stayed in place, polluting the reef waters, until the U.S. government removed them in 2014.

Atoll of Evil?

Just where in the world did the crew and wreckage of the whaling ship that crashed on Palmyra go? Did the atoll swallow them whole? The investigators of this missing shipwreck weren't the only ones to wonder. In fact, some people wonder if the entire atoll could be under an evil curse.

Cursed with Danger?

If any of the whaling ship's crew had survived the shipwreck, sharks might have gotten them. Sailors report that Palmyra's sea and lagoon are full of gray and blacktip sharks. And that might not be the only danger that curses the place. In 1870, the *Angel* struck one of Palmyra's reefs. Though some of the crew made it to shore, they didn't survive. When another ship stopped at the island, they found the crew's bodies scattered everywhere. Someone or something had savagely murdered them. But just who or what and why remains a mystery.

Sailors have feared Palmyra Atoll ever since its discovery. Many tales have been told of sharks and mysterious sea monsters that threaten anyone who sails near.

Get Me Out of Here

Even the air on Palmyra Island seems to be cursed. It gets to shipwrecked sailors and visitors alike. Some say the air feels heavy with a "sense of doom" that grows worse the longer they stay there. This dread becomes terrifying for some people. When the U.S. Navy had a base of operations there in World War II, some soldiers and sailors demanded to leave the island. Others had panic attacks. Still others became violent. Fights broke out, and people were murdered.

Palmyra's heavy air even seems to affect planes. One patrol plane went down in a trail of smoke. A search party looked all over the island but found that the plane and its crew had vanished into the thick air. The navy reported it was "like they'd dropped off the edge of the earth."

MYSTERIOUS MURDERS

Mysterious murders have continued to occur on Palmyra Atoll in modern times. For example, in 1985, Duane Walker was convicted of murdering a rich American named Eleanor Graham on Palmyra. He also stole the yacht that belonged to her husband, Malcolm. Investigators found Eleanor's remains buried in a trunk in one of the lagoons. Although Walker admitted to shooting Malcolm, his body, like so many others, has never been found. This tale of murder and mystery was the subject of a best-selling book, *And the Sea Will Tell*, in 1991. A TV miniseries based on the book aired the same year.

Even today, visitors say they feel uneasy on Palmyra and look forward to leaving.

LOOK AT THE EVIDENCE

Some people say ghosts of shipwrecked sailors haunt Palmyra Atoll. Others say the atoll is a gateway to another world. Still others say it is a living being that wants to do evil. What evidence supports these theories? Is it convincing? What do you think?

GHOSTS OF THE BLACK DEATH

Many ghost hunters say tiny Poveglia Island off the coast of Italy near Venice is one of the most paranormally active places in the world. Some people have been so alarmed by what they've seen there that they pledge never to return.

DID YOU KNOW?

The term **quarantine** comes from the Italian words for 40 days. The Black Death was a **plague** that swept over Europe in the 1300s. Ships coming from infected ports had to sit in the harbor for 40 days to make sure there were no plague cases on board before anyone was allowed to enter the port.

Visitors Beware

Ghost hunters who visit Poveglia Island today find abandoned buildings that once served as plague hospitals and homes for the mentally ill. As well, the soil is mixed with human ash. The ash comes from the remains of thousands of people who died there of the plague in the 1700s. The government burned their bodies to stop the spread of the infectious disease.

Even doctors looked scary during plague times because of the masks they wore for protection. The pointed beak was filled with sponges soaked in vinegar and pleasant smelling herbs. The doctors believed that breathing through such "gas masks" could stop the spread of plague.

Poveglia is a small island located near Venice, Italy.

Ghostly Graveyard

Mass graves of plague victims lie all over the island. Over time, wind and rain have exposed skulls and bones from some of the graves. The island has been featured on at least two TV series: *Ghost Adventures* and *Scariest Places on Earth*. The *Ghost Adventures* crew reported that their equipment stopped working as soon as they reached the island. Even so, they were still able to capture footage of the show's host trying to fend off an attack from an invisible ghost!

Other visitors have reported seeing the ghost of a doctor. According to legend, he did experiments on his mentally ill patients. Locals also report hearing the bell chime from an old church tower, even though the bell disappeared long ago.

LOOK AT THE EVIDENCE

Evidence for Poveglia Island being haunted comes from eyewitnesses and TV footage. The island is uninhabited and overgrown. Could natural ***phenomena*** *cause some of the sights and sounds reported? Though the TV footage shows the host of the show being attacked by a ghost, the ghost is not visible. Is the evidence convincing? What do you think?*

SHIPS OF DEATH

The worst plague epidemic in European history began in 1347, when 12 trading ships from the Black Sea docked at the port of Messina, Italy. Most of the sailors on the ships were already dead. The bodies of the survivors were covered with black boils that oozed blood and pus.

The sailors were infected with the Black Death. From Messina, the plague spread like wildfire. Over the next five years, the disease killed about 20 million people in Europe. It wiped out nearly one-third of the continent's population.

There were no ghosts on those ships, only dead and dying people. The fear of the Black Death, however, haunted the people of Europe for many years. In this case the fear was real. No one knew then how the Black Death was passed on from one person to another. There seemed to be no rational explanation. Today, we know the plague is caused by a type of bacteria that can be spread by fleas from infected rats.

INTO THE DOOM AT FULL SAIL

No one knows why Her Majesty's Ship (HMS) *Eurydice* sank off the coast of the Isle of Wight, an island off the coast of England, in 1878. The 26-gun Royal Navy frigate (see below) had just crossed the Atlantic Ocean and was in tip-top shape. As she zipped past the island at full sail with her ports open, a raging snowstorm blew in.

The Eurydice *was built for speed. Its hull was designed to allow it to sail through shallow waters.*

We're Sunk, Mates

The snow created whiteout conditions. After 10 minutes, the *Eurydice* had almost sunk. Only its **masts** and **topsails** were still visible. Of the 317 crew members and trainees on board, many went down with the ship. Others died in the freezing waters. Only two sailors survived, which made this one of the worst peacetime disasters in British naval history. Is it any wonder the ghost of the *Eurydice* has haunted the shore ever since?

A frigate is a small warship with a single deck of guns. Frigates specialized in coastal patrols and supporting larger vessels.

Ghost Ship Clips In

The day of the disaster, Sir John MacNeill startled friends at lunch near London by blurting out, "Good heavens! Why don't they close the portholes and reef the sails?" MacNeill said he'd had a vision of a ship racing up the English Channel in full sail with her **gunports** open. Later, sailors and fishermen began seeing a ghost ship off the Isle of Wight. In the 1930s, a submarine captain spotted a three-mast ship heading straight for the sub at full sail. Once the captain changed course to avoid a collision, the ghost ship was gone. In 1998, Prince Edward of the British royal family said he saw a three-mast ship while in the same area filming a segment for the TV series *Crown and Country*. The crew even said they caught the ghost ship on film.

GHOST TALK

In 2013, a British newspaper, the *Daily Mail*, ran a story about a ghost ship in the United States. There had been many previous reports of strange events on the USS *Hornet*, a retired aircraft carrier in San Francisco Bay. This time, a group of ghostbusters said they had an audio recording. The ghosts seemed to be information techs who tapped out a message in **Morse code**. The message was simple. It just said, "Hi, I.T."

The Hornet *is now a naval museum. It is docked in Alameda, California.*

LOOK AT THE EVIDENCE

A number of eyewitnesses say they have evidence of the Eurydice ghost ship. They include the film crew who say they captured footage of it. What is unusual is how many eyewitnesses say they've seen a ship with three masts and open gunports. But some people say the image of the ghost ship is caused by freaky reflections of light on mist. And when the film crew went to view the footage, it jammed in the machine. Is the ghost ship for real? What do you think?

RETURN OF THE GHOST SHIP

Now here's a haunting tale of love, murder, and revenge on the open sea. The day before Valentine's Day in 1748, the sailing ship *Lady Lovibond* set sail for Portugal from England. Not more than six miles off the coast, disaster struck.

Honeymoon Haunt

Captain Simon Reed had arranged the voyage as a honeymoon for his beautiful bride, Annetta. Little did he know, or so the legend goes, that his first mate, John Rivers, also had a crush on his bride. As the captain, Annetta, and the crew celebrated below deck, a fit of jealous rage overcame Rivers. After attacking the first officer, he steered the ship onto the Goodwin Sands, a deadly area of shifting sandbars in the English Channel. Soon the *Lady Lovibond* joined thousands of other ships that had wrecked on the sandbars. Everybody on board was killed.

An old superstition said it was bad luck to bring a woman aboard a ship. Some people thought Captain Reed paid the price for ignoring it. But the many women sailing today know there is no truth to it!

Many Ghostly Returns

On February 13, 1798, exactly 50 years after the *Lady Lovibond* wrecked on the Goodwin Sands, something strange happened in the same area. James Westlake, captain of the *Edenbridge*, was edging around the sandbars. He was surprised to see a three-masted ship coming straight toward his ship. Westlake had to turn his ship's wheel hard to avoid a collision. Rescue crews raced to the area, but they found no trace of the phantom ship. Fifty years later, the *Lady* surfaced again, and again 50 years after that, in 1898. Then in 1948, Captain Bull Prestwick reported a sighting so vivid he said the ship appeared to be real. On February 13, 1998, a crowd gathered to watch, but the ship did not materialize. Is she resting in peace, or will she return in 2048?

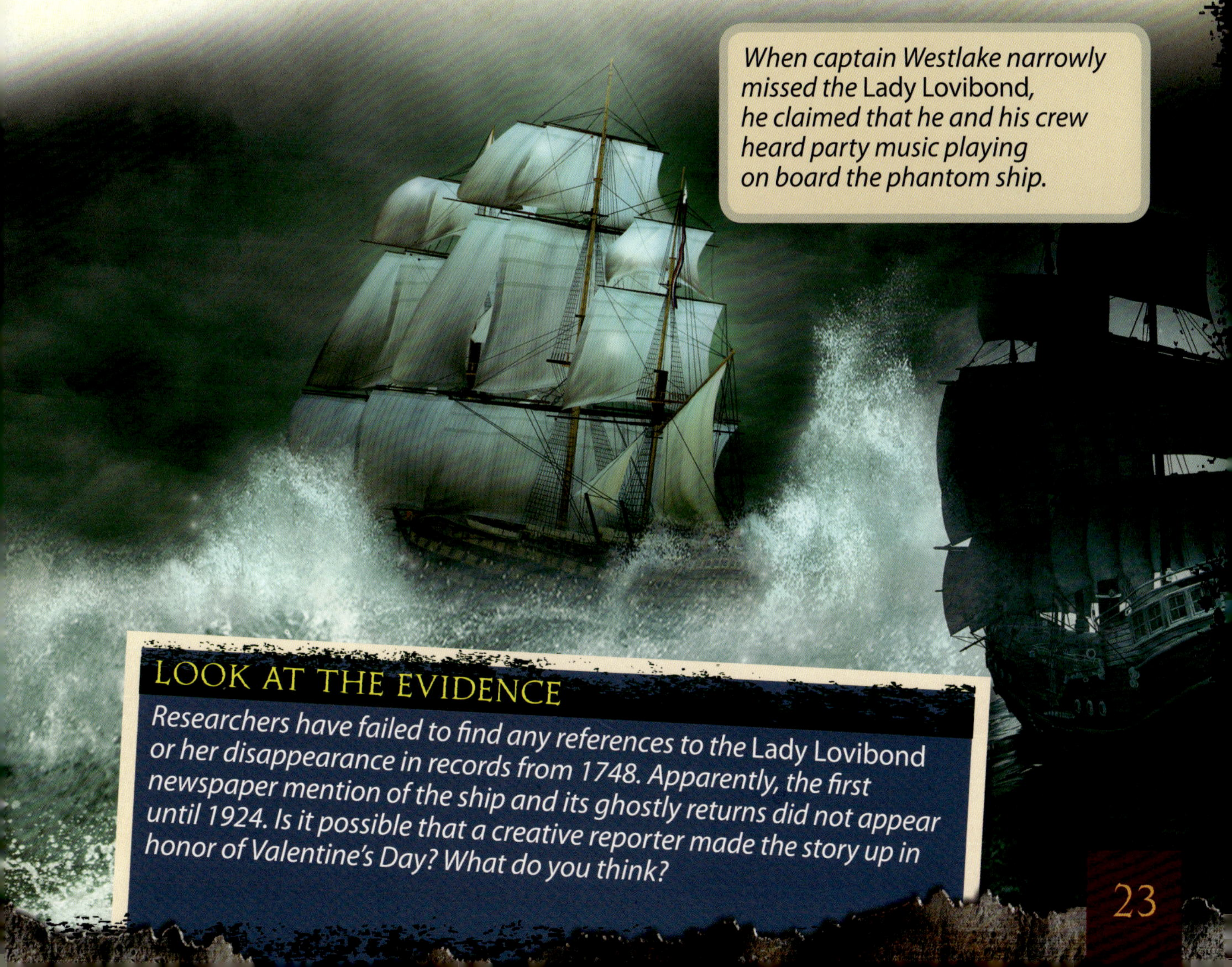

When captain Westlake narrowly missed the Lady Lovibond*, he claimed that he and his crew heard party music playing on board the phantom ship.*

LOOK AT THE EVIDENCE

Researchers have failed to find any references to the Lady Lovibond *or her disappearance in records from 1748. Apparently, the first newspaper mention of the ship and its ghostly returns did not appear until 1924. Is it possible that a creative reporter made the story up in honor of Valentine's Day? What do you think?*

CURSE OF THE FLYING DUTCHMAN

The legend of the *Flying Dutchman* ghost ship has haunted sailors around the world for more than 300 years. According to the most popular version of the story, the Dutch captain Hendrik van der Decken and his crew of living skeletons are doomed to sail the seven seas forever. Anyone who sees van der Decken's ghost ship will die a swift and horrible death.

DID YOU KNOW?

If this ghost ship story sounds familiar to you, there's good reason for that. It inspired the *Pirates of the Caribbean* movies and a *SpongeBob SquarePants* character. Earlier, Sir Arthur Conan Doyle based a short story about Sherlock Holmes on the legend.

The tale of the Flying Dutchman *quickly spread all over the world. It is perhaps the most well-known legend of the sea.*

Captain Gone Wild

The story begins in 1641, when van der Decken tried to sail his ship through the stormy waters around the Cape of Good Hope at the southern tip of Africa. Fearing for their lives, passengers begged him to change course and the crew rose up against the Dutch captain. But van der Decken stuck to his guns in more ways than one. He shot the rebel leader in cold blood, threw his body overboard, and continued sailing through the stormy sea.

Keepers of the Cape Point Lighthouse in South Africa say they have seen the Flying Dutchman *during violent storms like the one that destroyed the ship.*

ARCTIC GHOST SHIP

In 1931, a ship called the *Baychimo* got trapped in Arctic ice. Then a blizzard struck. When the storm lifted three days later, the ship had vanished. The crew, who had taken shelter on shore for the winter, thought the ship had sunk. Days later, the *Baychimo* appeared miles away. The crew boarded her to get supplies. Shortly after, the ship vanished again. Inuit hunters and traders experienced the same phenomenon when the *Baychimo* appeared elsewhere. 1969 marks the ghost ship's last recorded sighting. No wreck has ever been found. Do you think the ship will be spotted again?

The Baychimo *traveled along the northern coast of Canada to collect animal pelts from trading posts and bring supplies to Inuit villages. The ship was owned by the Hudson Bay Company.*

Close Encounters

Despite van der Decken's courage, the storm destroyed his ship. The disaster gave rise to the legend that the ghostly reappearance of the ship would doom any who saw it. Even so, several people are convinced that they have seen the *Flying Dutchman* and lived to tell the tale. For example, in 1881, young Prince George of England, who would became King George V, recorded a sighting of the ghost ship off the coast of Australia. The prince's brother and 13 other crewmen also saw the ghostly vessel pass by. Hours later, the first sailor to report the sighting fell from his perch on the tall mast. He "was smashed to atoms" on the deck.

As a teen, King George V traveled the world with the British Navy. He recorded a sighting of the Flying Dutchman *early one morning off the coast of Australia: "A strange red light as of a phantom ship all aglow."*

Almost everyone who saw the Flying Dutchman *said that the ship glowed with a spooky light. Does this support the idea that these sightings involved a mirage?*

Just a Mirage?

Today, scientists say the *Flying Dutchman* is just a mirage, or a trick of light. A mirage can happen at sea when sunlight heats the upper air, leaving a cooler area just above the water. Objects far enough away to be out of sight below the horizon then reflect the light in such a way that it refracts, or bends. This bending of the light can make unseen objects appear to be floating upside down above the horizon.

Some accounts link the Flying Dutchman *to a real sea captain named Bernard Fokke. He sailed for the Dutch East India Company. Fokke was famous for his speedy trips between Holland and Indonesia. In fact, he traveled so quickly that some people said he must have made a pact with the devil.*

MYSTERY OF THE MARY CELESTE

There was something about the *Mary Celeste* that made sailors wonder if the ship might be cursed. Maybe it was that her first captain died two days after taking the **helm**. Or that she plowed into a fishing boat on her first voyage. In 1872, the *Dei Gratia* crew found her drifting off the coast of the Azores. The captain sent a boarding party to offer help. They found charts scattered about, the crew's belongings intact, a pump that had been taken apart, and a six-month stash of food and water. The only things missing were the lifeboat, passengers, and crew. Just what happened to them is still a mystery.

LOOK AT THE EVIDENCE

What evidence is there that the ghost of the Flying Dutchman haunts the sea? What do eyewitness accounts reveal? Did eyewitnesses see something paranormal in action or just a mirage (see above)? What do you think?

WHAT DO YOU THINK?

Is the Bermuda Triangle haunted? Do ghost ships appear and disappear on the seven seas? Is Palmyra Atoll truly cursed? Is Poveglia Island a place of pure evil? And is the *Flying Dutchman* doomed to sail the seven seas forever?

Unsolved Mysteries of the Sea

Now that you've had a chance to consider some of the evidence for the haunted-at-sea cases in this book, what do you think? Keep an open mind as you think about each one. Many ghost stories, haunted places, and fantastical sea creatures are hoaxes created to attract attention or get people to visit places. But some strange goings-on still have no logical explanation. The cause may be unknown paranormal forces or phenomena that science has yet to discover.

DID YOU KNOW?

Cursed or not, some places seem to have a negative effect on anyone who goes near. The cause may be a kind of negative energy that exists in nature. Animals seem to have a special sense of such spots. They seek out some and avoid others. If our pets could tell us what they sense, we might learn a lot about invisible natural forces!

Many ghost stories tell of ships whose crews are skeletons. It must take paranormal force to move bones without any muscles!

Paranormal Paradox

How do you "prove" the existence of any kind of paranormal activity? The problem is, you can't. By its very definition, the paranormal is hard to explain logically. Because of that, an occurence cannot be confirmed as paranormal through science. If it could be, it would not fit the definition anymore. Can we use science to prove the existence of wormholes? In science fiction, they are gateways to other times and places. Today this is impossible, but what discoveries might we make in the future?

PRIZE MONEY AVAILABLE!

If you can ever prove that you have paranormal powers or that you've observed some kind of supernatural activity, you may be able to make some money. The James Randl Educational Foundation will pay a million dollars to anyone who can prove their powers under strict test conditions. Also, the Independent Investigations Group offers a $100,000 prize to anyone who can prove paranormal activity under controlled testing. So far, no one has been able to do it. Could you be the first to win a prize?

The FeeJee mermaid was the most famous of several fake mermaids displayed during the 1800s.

FAMOUS HOAXES

P. T. BARNUM'S FEEJEE MERMAID

Want to see a genuine mermaid? Come on down to the American Museum of Natural History. In 1842, P.T. Barnum, an American showman, ran newspaper ads to draw people to see the FeeJee (as Fiji was known at the time) mermaid. The museum exhibit was one of the most spectacular hoaxes of all time. Barnum claimed that a naturalist, Dr. J. Griffin, had caught the mermaid near the island of Feejee. Thousands of people flocked to see the stuffed dead specimen. If anyone thought something was fishy, they were right. Japanese fishermen had stitched together the FeeJee mermaid from the head and torso of a monkey and the tail of a fish. Even the naturalist, Dr. Griffin, was a fake.

LEARNING MORE

BOOKS

Ghosts at Sea, by Lisa Owens, Bellwether Media Inc., 2016.

Hauntings at Sea: Real Haunted Ships, Oceans, and Beaches, by Zachary Knowles, True Ghost Stories, 2017.

Jr. Graphic Mysteries: The Bermuda Triangle: The Disappearance of Flight 19, by Jack DeMolay, Rosen Publishing Group, 2007.

The Mary Celeste: An Unsolved Mystery from History, by Jane Yolen and Heidi Elisabet Yolen Stemple, Simon & Schuster Books for Young Readers, 1999.

The Unexplained: The Bermuda Triangle, by Adam Stone, Bellwether Media Inc., 2011.

WEBSITES

Abandoned Ship: The Mary Celeste

www.smithsonianmag.com/history/abandoned-ship-the-mary-celeste-174488104/

Bermuda Triangle: Beyond the Intrigue

https://news.nationalgeographic.com/news/2002/12/1205_021205_bermudatriangle.html

Historic Mysteries: The Ghost Ship Lady Lovibond

www.historicmysteries.com/lady-lovibond

The Mysterious Disappearance of Flight 19

www.history.com/news/the-mysterious-disappearance-of-flight-19

GLOSSARY

Age of Discovery The period from around 1400 to 1600, in which Europeans traveled the rest of the world in search for new lands

Atlantis Mythical island in the Atlantic Ocean that, according to legend, sank beneath the sea

atoll A ring-shaped reef, island, or chain of islands made of coral

coral reef Large underwater structure in warm oceans made up of the skeletons of coral—marine animals without spines

crustacean Member of a large class of mostly water-dwelling arthropods, such as lobsters, shrimps, crabs

curse Words intended to cause harm or punishment on someone or something

demon An evil spirit or devil that may exist on its own or within a person

evidence Available facts, eyewitness reports, and objects that support whether a belief or theory is true

eyewitness A person who has seen something happen and can describe it

gunport Hole in the side of a ship for guns to shoot out from

helm Wheel and other equipment for steering a ship

Incas South American Native peoples who established an empire in Peru before the Spanish conquest

legend An old or traditional story that may or may not be seen as factual but cannot be proven true

leviathan A big sea monster

magnetic field A space near a magnetic body where magnetic forces can be detected

mast A post on a boat carrying a sail

mermaid A mythical sea creature with the head and body of a woman and the tail of a fish

mineral ore a type of rock that contains minerals that can be refined and used in industries

Morse code A method of sending messages using an alphabet in which letters are represented by combinations of long and short signals of light or sound

myth A traditional story, usually about supernatural beings or events

paranormal Things or events that cannot be explained through normal scientific understanding

phenomena Facts or situations seen to exist, especially those whose cause or explanation are unknown

plague A contagious disease that is caused by bacteria, spreads quickly, and can kill many people

port A town or city with a harbor where ships load and unload

quarantine A time period during which people or animals are kept away from others to make sure they don't spread an infectious disease

theory An idea that explains something or a situation

topsail A sail set above another sail

typhoon A tropical storm occurring especially in the region of the Indian or western Pacific Oceans

waterspout A tornado that forms over water

INDEX